Brotha Boy

By Timiah Shillingsworth

Library For All Ltd.

Library For All is an Australian not for profit organisation with a mission to make knowledge accessible to all via an innovative digital library solution. Visit us at libraryforall.org

Brotha Boy

First published 2023

Published by Library For All Ltd
Email: info@libraryforall.org
URL: libraryforall.org

Our Yarning logo design by Jason Lee, Bidjipidji Art

Original illustrations by Michael Magpantay

Brotha Boy
Shillingsworth, Timiah
ISBN: 978-1-923063-99-0
SKU03350

Brotha Boy

We respect and honour Aboriginal and Torres Strait Islander Elders past, present and future. We acknowledge the stories, traditions and living cultures of Aboriginal and Torres Strait Islander peoples on this land and commit to building a brighter future together.

Matai lives in a small town, out bush among the mulga and red dirt. He loves to play sports such as football, soccer, swimming, and boxing.

Matai has many hobbies like hanging out with his friends, playing games on PlayStation, and going down the river with his kayak.

Matai was born without his right arm, but it never stops him from doing the things he loves.

When Matai was in school, he was very excited to compete in the school's swimming carnival day as he was a strong swimmer.

Matai was on a winning streak, winning several races, but he was very nervous to do the butterfly, as he thought the stroke was too tricky to swim.

Luckily, his mum and family were there to help boost his confidence. Mum shouted, "Come on bub, I know you can do it. You swim strong down the river!"

Matai's race was up next. He jumped up onto the starting block and got in starting position. Then, "BANG!" Off he went.

He struggled at first, but after a few kicks and arm strokes he got the rhythm.

As his head popped up out of the water, his sister yelled out, "Come on Brotha Boy, you got this!"

Matai swam harder and faster and with a big effort, he won the race!

As he got out of the water, his family gave him the biggest hug, and the teachers congratulated him.

Matai grinned and accepted all the ribbons he had won in the different stroke races.

"See, Brotha Boy, we knew you'd win," said his family.

You can use these questions to talk about this book with your family, friends and teachers.

What did you learn from this book?

Describe this book in one word. Funny? Scary? Colourful? Interesting?

How did this book make you feel when you finished reading it?

What was your favourite part of this book?

download our reader app
getlibraryforall.org

About the author

Timiah was born in Charleville, Queensland, and is from the Bidjara Nation. She now lives in Canberra. Timiah and her family love Christmas. Her favourite book when she was younger was *Goosebumps*.

Timiah's brother Matai won't let anything stop him.

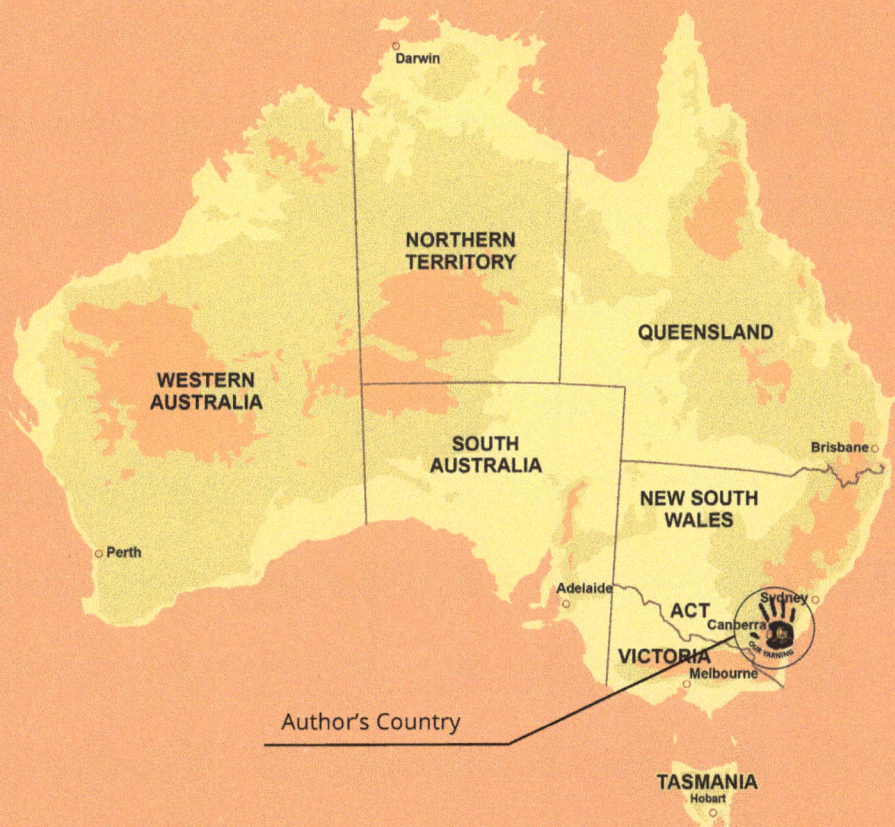

Darwin

NORTHERN
TERRITORY

QUEENSLAND

WESTERN
AUSTRALIA

SOUTH
AUSTRALIA

Brisbane

NEW SOUTH
WALES

Perth

Adelaide

Sydney

ACT
Canberra

VICTORIA

Melbourne

Author's Country

TASMANIA
Hobart

Our Yarning

Want to discover more books from this collection? Our Yarning is a collection of books written by Aboriginal and Torres Strait Islander peoples across Australia.

We know that children learn better, and enjoy reading more, when they see themselves in the stories, characters and illustrations of the books they read.

To download the app, visit the Google Play Store on any Android device and search 'Our Yarning'.

libraryforall.org

www.ingramcontent.com/pod-product-compliance
Lightning Source LLC
Chambersburg PA
CBHW042346040426
42448CB00019B/3423